IN HER OWN TIME

ANNIE BESANT

Olivia Bennett

Hamish Hamilton
London

IN HER OWN TIME

This series focuses a spotlight on women whose lives and work have all too often been overlooked yet who have made significant contributions to society in many different areas: from politics and painting to science and social reform.

Women's voices have in the past been the silent ones of history. In Britain, for example, the restrictions of society, the time-consuming nature of domestic work, and the poor educational opportunities available to women until this century, have meant that not only did women rarely have the opportunity to explore their abilities beyond those which society expected of them, but also that their aspirations and achievements were often not recorded.

This series profiles a number of women who, through a combination of character and circumstance, were able to influence ideas and attitudes or contribute to the arts and sciences. None of them were alone in their ambitions. There must have been many other women whose experiences we know nothing of because they were not recorded. Many of the 'ordinary' women who have supported the so-called 'exceptional' women of history also displayed great courage, skill and determination. Political and social change, in particular, has been accelerated by the pioneering work of individual women but rarely achieved without the collective efforts of masses of unknown women.

The work of many women in the series took them into the public eye: some were honoured and celebrated, more frequently they faced disapproval or lack of sympathy with their ideas. Many were ahead of their time and only later did their pioneering activities gain public respect. Others found their lives so deeply entangled with current events that their path was virtually chosen for them. A few were not closely involved with contemporary society but highly original characters who nevertheless influenced or informed others. By exploring the struggles, hopes, failures and achievements of these women, we can discover much about the society they lived in and how each made their personal contribution — in their own way, in their own time.

Olivia Bennett

HAMISH HAMILTON CHILDREN'S BOOKS
Penguin Books Ltd, 27 Wrights Lane, London W8 5TZ (Publishing & Editorial)
and Harmondsworth, Middlesex, England (Distribution & Warehouse)
Viking Penguin Inc., 40 West 23rd Street, New York, New York 10010, U.S.A.
Penguin Books Australia Ltd, Ringwood, Victoria, Australia
Penguin Books Canada Ltd, 2801 John Street, Markham, Ontario, Canada L3R 1B4
Penguin Books (N.Z.) Ltd, 182–190 Wairau Road, Auckland 10, New Zealand

First published in Great Britain 1988 by
Hamish Hamilton Children's Books
Copyright © 1988 by Olivia Bennett

Design by Sally Boothroyd
Cover design by Clare Truscott

British Library Cataloguing in Publication Data
Bennett, Olivia
Annie Besant.—(In her own time).
1. Besant, Annie—Juvenile literature
2. Theosophists—Great Britain—
Biography—Juvenile literature   3. Social
reformers—Great Britain—Biography—
Juvenile literature
1. Title   II. Series
326'.924   BP585.B3
ISBN 0-241-12224-4

Filmset in Palatino by
Katerprint Typesetting Services, Oxford
Printed in Great Britain by
Butler & Tanner Ltd, Frome, Somerset

Contents

Chapter One

The Many Lives of Annie Besant

Annie Besant was a pioneer and supporter of many different causes. So much so that people have always found it hard to understand how one person could deal with such a wide range of ideas and activities. No wonder one of her biographers called his books on her *The First Five Lives of Annie Besant* and *The Last Four Lives of Annie Besant*. When she died, aged eighty-five in 1933 in India, she had fought for greater freedom or justice in almost every area of life you can think of: marriage, working conditions, the law, science, religion, motherhood, birth control, poverty, education and politics. Much of this work was done in the first forty years of her life. Most of the second half of her life was spent in India, fighting for Indian people's rights and, above all, devoted to the religion of Theosophy. Her Theosophical beliefs brought her spiritual peace but tried the patience and understanding of many of her earlier friends and admirers. They found them difficult to reconcile with Annie the social reformer. Annie represents different things to different people — but most would agree that she was, by any standards, a quite remarkable person.

She was certainly a very brave woman. She grew up in the Victorian world, in which a woman's role was to support and cherish her husband and family — and to do little else. Annie broke all her society's rules about a woman's place by leaving her husband,

Annie spent much of the second half of her life removed from the battles for social reform which she had spear-headed until her forties. Thereafter she lived mostly in India, fighting for its right to self-government and running the Theosophical Society. She felt India was her spiritual home and adopted many of its traditions and customs, including loose, comfortable clothing.

During her eighty-five years Annie Besant lived many lives, all of them full . . . many of them so different they could have belonged to utterly different people . . .

a free-thinker, a radical agitator, a feminist, a crusader for birth control, author-editor-publisher, a convert to Fabian socialism, a teacher of science, a social reformer, a strike leader and a trade unionist . . . she eventually became the international President of the stormy and mystical Theosophical Society . . . and in India, a religious, educational and political leader.

A. *Nethercot*, The First Five Lives of Annie Besant (1960)

earning her own living, taking a degree, speaking out about birth control, giving up Christianity and campaigning publicly for social reforms. For although the country was ruled by a woman and although Queen Victoria (1819–1901) was one of the world's most respected monarchs, the Victorian age was one of the most stifling and restrictive periods of modern history for women.

The second sex

When Annie was born, in 1847, a woman had practically no legal rights. Once she married any property or land she had belonged to her husband. Any money she earned — and even her children — belonged to him. Women could not take a degree or vote. And although there were no actual laws against women being independent and earning their own living, in practice it was almost impossible for middle-class women like Annie. Girls of 'good family' were expected to see marriage as their sole ambition. Their education was directed at giving them the skills and accomplishments to attract a husband. Most opportunities for training or further study were open only to men.

If it was unusual for middle or upper-class women to work, poorer women usually had no choice. Working-class men rarely earned enough to keep their families fed and clothed. The jobs open to these women were generally poorly paid and unskilled. Conditions were often unhealthy, sometimes dangerous. Trade unions were still quite rare and were mainly for skilled male workers. Women were paid less than men, even for the same work. Unmarried women usually worked as domestic servants in the homes of the better-off.

This sounds a harsh and unfair world, and in many ways it was, but the reality was not always so bad. Although the Victorian ideal was that the husband was the dominant partner, some marriages were in practice more equal relationships. Women with supportive husbands, fathers or brothers might be given the freedom and money to have satisfying lives of their own. But this depended entirely on good luck rather than on any legally held rights. If the men in a woman's life wished to treat her as the law and custom allowed, her world could be very limited. Annie's own marriage was not a happy one, and she discovered painfully soon just how little power she had compared with her husband. The Victorian era was, however, one of great change. By the time of Annie's death, the position of women, particularly in law, education and employment, had improved. Some of these changes were due in part to her.

The Strike Committee of the Match Makers' Union. One of the most famous episodes in Annie's life was her organisation of the successful Match Girls' Strike in 1888. It was the beginning of proper union representation for women and encouraged all unskilled workers to fight for better conditions.

Childhood

Annie Wood was born in London, but was three-quarters Irish. She was a very lively and rather precocious child, full of imagination and dreams. Her family was middle-class and fairly comfortably off but when her father died her mother was left in a difficult financial situation. Annie was only five and within a few months her younger brother, who had been sickly ever since her father's death, also died. Fortunately, various wealthier uncles and aunts helped Annie's mother through this sad time. They agreed to pay for the education of Annie's older brother Harry. Mrs Wood moved the family to Harrow, where he was sent to school. Although Annie was an exceptionally intelligent child, no relatives thought her education very important. She might have

Looking at this picture of Annie as a young girl it is hard to imagine that she was to become a woman who questioned or defied the conventions of her society on almost every important issue of the time.

suffered the usual undemanding school that was considered appropriate for girls at the time but she was lucky. When she was eight a Miss Marryat, friend of a family friend, kindly offered to educate her at her Dorset home. It meant leaving her mother, whom Annie adored, but fortunately she loved the lessons and came home every holiday.

Ellen Marryat's small school was not typical of the time. She did not believe in learning by heart, so that you could repeat information like a parrot but might not understand it. Nor did she believe in endless spelling and grammar lessons. She taught her pupils to write their own compositions about things which interested them, and to learn good English that way. Above all, she expected her pupils to think clearly and to think for themselves, in an age when most women were taught to agree with what men thought. Annie owed a lot to this style of teaching. She had a sharp intelligent mind and did think things through for herself, but she was lucky to have been encouraged in this from the beginning.

Miss Marryat was intensely religious, as was Mrs Wood, and so at school and home there was a strong religious atmosphere. Throughout her life, when Annie believed in something she believed in it passionately and so she concentrated most of her spare time and energy on reading and studying the scriptures. She daydreamed of performing great Christian deeds against the forces of evil or of becoming a famous martyr like Joan of Arc. It was all very innocent but rather serious. Novels and going to the theatre were disapproved of as 'frivolous'. Annie herself, in her autobiography, admitted that she was a bit of a 'little prig' at the time.

I would spend many hours in daydreams . . . But, always with a shock, I was brought back to earth, where there were no heroic deeds to do, no lions to face, no judges to defy . . . no chance of preaching and suffering for a new religion.

Annie Besant,
An Autobiography (1893)

11

Chapter Two

Further Education

. . . all that was deepest and truest in my nature chafed against my useless days, longed for work, yearned to devote itself, as I had read women saints had done, to the service of the church and the poor, to the battling against sin and misery . . .

Annie Besant,
An Autobiography

At sixteen Annie left Miss Marryat's private school and came home. She was unusually well educated for a girl of her time but in spite of her obvious cleverness, there could be no question of going to university. She spent her time reading books in French and German, pouring over scholarly works, English poetry, philosophy and above all books on religion. She did occasionally break away from these serious pursuits and went to dances, where she met many of her brother's friends. She was small, dark and pretty and many of the boys were attracted to her. But Annie was not romantic about people, only about being a martyr or some sort of religious heroine. It was perhaps partly because she was so unaware of men as romantic companions, that she found herself at eighteen engaged to be married almost without realising it.

She had met Frank Besant in London a few times and again on a family seaside holiday. He was a shy, rather stiff and unrelaxed young man, who was studying to be a clergyman. They had only known each other a short time when he proposed. Annie was so surprised she did not know what to say. Frank took the awkward silence to mean yes. After he left, Annie felt utterly miserable. When she confessed to her mother what had happened, Mrs Wood was not too happy either. She sent Annie away to stay with the Roberts, friends in Manchester, and they took her off on a trip to Switzerland.

Annie loved her travels but returned home to find the situation unchanged. She simply did not have the courage to break off her engagement and it was announced officially. Later she was to admit how 'out of sheer weakness and fear of inflicting pain, I drifted into an engagement with a man I did not pretend to love'. It was to prove a dreadful mistake. At the time the only romantic view Annie could take of the situation was to see her future self as a sort of saintly vicar's wife, giving comfort to the sad, charity to the poor and nursing the sick back to health. This appealed greatly to her passionate desire to devote herself to good works, but it proved to be quite unrealistic.

Frank and Annie were engaged for some time. Once Annie tried to break it off, but her mother was horrified. 'Would I, her daughter, break my word . . . ? She could be stern where honour was concerned, that sweet mother of mine, and I yielded to her wish.' During these months Annie made two

'The Sunday School Teacher'
Annie's childhood, like most of her contemporaries', was full of visits to church and Sunday School. Influenced by her intensely religious mother and teacher, she became a particularly fervent Christian, who dreamed of becoming a religious martyr.

Annie's upbringing had shielded her from the realities of life for the many people in Victorian Britain who lived in slums like these. When she visited Manchester, aged nineteen, her friends the Roberts opened her eyes to the poverty and injustice in her society.

important discoveries about politics and religion. They stirred up the first feelings of concern about the issues to which she was later to devote her life.

Religious doubts

First of all, she suffered a slight loss of confidence in her religion. During Holy Week that year, she sat down to write a history of the events which took place in that week leading up to Easter. She compared the four Gospels of the Bible. To her horror she discovered that the Gospels did not tell the story with exactly the same details. Today it is perhaps hard to imagine just how shocking this could be. Remember that Annie was a deeply religious person, who believed in the truth of the Bible's every word. For many Christians the importance of the Gospels was that they were written by disciples whose concern was to get across the inner meaning of Jesus' story, rather than just the historical facts. They wanted their readers to understand the power of Jesus and his message. But Annie's nature needed exact truths and facts. Her discovery sowed the first seed of doubt about Christianity in her mind. She couldn't bear to think about it too much at the time. As she said, 'I smothered it up, buried it, and smoothed the turf over its grave.'

Poverty and politics

The other experience sparked off the beginning of her political and social interests. Visiting the Roberts again in Manchester, she spent a lot of time with the elderly husband, William. He was a lawyer who had often worked, unpaid, on behalf of the city's working people. He was a much loved figure in the local slums and mining districts. He taught Annie what life was really like for these people. Up to then, she had thought of 'the poor' as unfortunates, people to whom one gave charity, kindness and pity. William Roberts made her see their courage and hard work, their dignity and pride. He told her how women Annie's age used to work in the mines, half-naked, pulling along heavy weights in damp and dangerous conditions. It was tough work and mine workers became old and worn out long before their time. Small children were put to work, too. Wages were so low that families were desperate for

William Roberts described to Annie how until recently many a girl of her own age spent all day underground in the mines, hauling coal trucks, and how he had campaigned to make this 'foul, brutalising' employment illegal.

Coal-mining woman, 1842.

every penny they could get. Babies of three or four were left to stand guard by a pit door and keep it open. It was a frightening experience being left alone in a dark, dripping underground corridor. Often they fell asleep during the long hours with nothing to do and would be kicked awake by some angry miner who had found the door shut.

The work and words of William Roberts made a deep impression on Annie. Under his guidance, she began to feel that what working people deserved was not charity, but justice. They were not parasites on the rich but producers of wealth. If they received decent wages for the coal they dug, cloth they wove, food they grew, bricks they made — they wouldn't need charity. If the conditions they lived and worked in were better, they would not suffer frequent sickness and injury.

At the end of her stay Annie witnessed an event which she never forgot. It seemed to underline some of the lessons about injustice which she had recently learnt. Three young Irishmen were sentenced to death for resistance against the police. They supported an Ireland free from British rule and had been on a fund-raising trip to England when they were arrested. There had been a fight, in which a policeman was accidently shot and killed. Roberts helped in the trial but with no success. Annie was in court when the death sentence was passed. It was a harrowing experience for a relatively naive and sheltered girl. Annie later wrote that her love of liberty and freedom really stemmed from that moment. 'Then the flame of passionate love of liberty burst out in my heart, and has never flickered since.'

Chapter Three

Marriage and disillusionment

After all this excitement Annie returned home to face the third important event of 1867 for her: marriage. It took place in December. Annie was twenty, but she had none of the wordly knowledge a twenty-year-old might have today. She knew almost nothing of close relationships between men and women. She had developed no friendships with men, having grown up without a father and largely separated from her brother. Apart from the recent months in Manchester, she had led a sheltered existence. Life with Mrs Marryat and her mother had been untroubled and pleasant, with Annie encouraged to read and study free from any domestic responsibilities.

She could not be the bride of heaven, and therefore became the bride of Mr Frank Besant. He was hardly an adequate substitute.

W. T. Stead: editor and friend

Annie's engagement photo. Her obsession with religion meant she idealised clergymen as 'chosen servants of the lord'. This, plus her innocence and ignorance of life, led her to make what was to be a disastrous marriage to the Reverend Frank Besant.

'My dreamy life, into which no knowledge of evil had been allowed to penetrate, in which I had been guarded from all pain, shielded from all anxiety, kept innocent on all questions of sex, was no preparation for married existence, and left me defenceless to face a rude awakening.'

Thus Annie, like many a Victorian bride, entered marriage in a state of almost total ignorance of what it involved — and it proved an unpleasant shock. In her autobiography she admits that from the wedding night onwards, their married life was tense and unhappy. They seem never to have been friends or to have really enjoyed each other's company. Frank was probably equally inexperienced at relationships and may well have felt insecure at the beginning, too. But he was not someone to talk over emotional matters. He was neither affectionate nor sympathetic. When problems arose he tried to escape them by being cold and distant.

Moreover, the Victorian view of marriage was that the man, as husband and father, was in charge. A wife should support his decisions and never question his judgement. And, as Annie later wrote, 'Frank had very high ideas of a husband's authority and a wife's submission.' Since Annie was clever, proud and quite hot-tempered, clashes between the two were frequent. She did not put all the blame on Frank. Many years later, in her autobiography, Annie wrote that she ought never to have married. She felt that her strong will, rebellious nature and 'fiery and passionate emotions' made her 'a most undesirable partner to sit in the lady's armchair on the domestic rug before the fire.'

The young couple moved to Cheltenham, where Frank had a teaching job. Annie began to get to know her neighbours. In a way, they only served to underline her loneliness, for the women 'talked to me only about babies and servants — troubles of which I knew nothing and which bored me unutterably.' Annie simply wasn't interested in housekeeping matters. She buried herself in her books and struggled to settle down into married life. She wrote some short stories

Many a middle-class Victorian bride entered marriage in a state of ignorance similar to Annie's. Expected to turn into self-sacrificing domestic angels, they also gave up any goods or property they had. Once she married, everything a women owned or earned belonged to her husband — even her children.

which to her great delight were published. It felt good to have some money of her own but the pleasure was short-lived. Frank took the fee himself, as was his legal right. Already Annie was having to face the harsh realities of being the unequal partner in the marriage.

Motherhood

In 1869 Annie and Frank had a son, Digby. Although Annie had not enjoyed pregnancy, she was thrilled with her baby and gained great pleasure from looking after him. Before she had time to really recover her health, she was pregnant again. A daughter, Mabel, was born in 1870. She was a delicate child and the following year became very ill with whooping cough. At one point it looked as though she was going to die. Annie sat up day and night nursing her. She found the pain and misery of her small baby almost unbearable. It was another test of her faith in God. She simply couldn't understand how He could let an innocent baby suffer so much. If God was truly full of mercy and love, how could He let her 'helpless, sinless babe' be 'tortured for weeks and left frail and suffering?'

Mabel eventually recovered but Annie's faith never gained its old strength. It was the beginning of the end of her life as a Christian. Her spiritual doubts had been made worse by her visits to sick and poor people in the neighbourhood. Instead of finding this a 'noble and uplifting experience', she was cast down by the misery she saw. The words of William Roberts came back to her; She was appalled at the injustice and cruelty in life.

It is perhaps hard for us to appreciate just how traumatic it was to lose one's religious faith in Annie's time. For somebody as passionate and spiritual as Annie it was particularly hard but for most Victorians it was unthinkable. The Church dominated society. Belief in God and Jesus Christ was passed on to children almost as soon as they were born. The Christian belief that there was life after death helped many a Victorian cope with sadness in life on Earth. Belief in God's infinite wisdom helped others develop compassion when faced with the suffering of others, instead of the anger and dismay it aroused in Annie. No wonder she tried hard to cling on to her beliefs. Annie wrote that there was 'no other pain so horrible' as to lose faith in God's love. It meant there was 'no gleam in the blackness of night; no voice to break the deadly silence; no hand outstretched to save.'

The gift of speech

It was to be three years before Annie gave up Christianity. Meanwhile her relationship with Frank got steadily worse. They moved to Lincolnshire and Frank became the vicar of Sibsey. The church and vicarage were beautiful but Annie was lonelier than ever in the tiny farming village. She flung herself into her books and looking after her children.

One day Annie discovered that she had a rare and powerful gift. Finding herself alone in the church, she locked the doors. Then she climbed up into the pulpit from where Frank would give his usually boring sermons — and gave one of her own. The pews were empty. Nobody was there to listen to her but Annie knew that she spoke exceptionally well. Her voice was strong yet musical, her words were clear and she was aware of a feeling of power. She was a natural speaker. In this age, before television or radio, public meetings were the most important means of

I shall never forget the feeling of power and delight — but mainly power — that came upon me as I sent my voice ringing down the aisles . . . none can know, save they who have felt it, what joy there is in the full rush of language that moves and sways, to feel a crowd respond to the lightest touch, to see faces brighten or darken at your bidding . . .

Annie Besant,
An Autobiography

spreading new ideas and exchanging views. The ability to speak well and carry a crowd was a tremendous advantage. Annie was to be famous later for her speeches.

In 1873, Annie and Frank separated. Annie was twenty-five. She had been finding life as a clergyman's wife increasingly difficult as her belief in Jesus weakened. The crisis came when she felt unable to take communion, an important ritual of Christian worship. Frank was furious and ordered her to take communion or leave. Their marriage had become very unhappy and they quarrelled often. Frank was sometimes violent. Annie decided to take a rare and desperate step for a woman of her time: she left her husband.

'In Church'
Annie's refusal to take communion, a central act of Christian worship, horrified Frank. Victorian society was built around an idealised picture of the family. A woman was to devote herself to supervising her husband's comfort and the Christian upbringing of their children. By rejecting this role, Annie scandalised her society.

Chapter 4

On Her Own

Annie and Frank drew up an arrangement. Digby was to stay with his father. Annie and Mabel were to live on a quarter of Frank's salary. This wasn't nearly enough. Annie searched desperately for work. Life for a Victorian woman on her own was hard. If she was middle-class, like Annie, there just weren't many jobs open to her. There were virtually no opportunities for training or higher education. And without the skills to earn a living, what choice had most women but to marry and be dependent on a man for their income?

At one point Annie was reduced to doing 'fancy needlework'. After five weeks of stitching she had earned five shillings (at a time when renting two rooms cost about £1 and 16 shillings a week). Fortunately she then got a temporary job as a governess, which also gave her somewhere to live. Annie had hoped to set up home with her mother but within a few months Mrs Wood fell ill and died. Annie felt her loss deeply. She loved her mother very much and now of all times needed her support and comfort.

This was one of the worst periods of Annie's life. She often went hungry. She made a bit of extra money writing pamphlets about Theism. Theism was a religious doctrine whose followers believed in God but not Jesus Christ. It was to Theism that Annie turned when she realised she could no longer be a member of the Christian Church.

Annie's religious questioning took her one

'The Family Governess'
This contemporary drawing illustrates the attitude to governesses at the time. It was a lonely, underpaid and undervalued job, yet one of the very few occupations open to a middle-class woman who needed to earn a living, as Annie found out when she left her husband.

step further, however. She became interested in the ideas of the National Secular Society. This was a group of people who believed in everyone's right to be free to think for themselves in political, religious and other matters. 'Freethinkers' rejected the Christian Church and for this reason they were thought to be a scandalous organisation by many Victorians. The Society had members all over England who met regularly in the Freethought Halls. The leading Freethinker was Charles Bradlaugh. In 1874 Annie went to hear him speak, having been told by various friends that he was one of the finest speakers in England and 'worth hearing whether one agreed with him or not'.

Annie found she did agree with him, and came away from his talk deeply impressed by the words — and the man. She became a Freethinker and started a long and deep friendship with Charles. He was a generous and thoughtful man, very intelligent and a natural leader. He came from a much poorer, less educated family than Annie did but he had taught himself law and become a

Where we differed, he never tried to override my judgement, nor force on me his views; we discussed all points of difference as equal friends.

Annie Besant
on Charles Bradlaugh

Charles Bradlaugh was a champion of people's rights, especially to hold their own political and religious beliefs. He was elected an MP. As a non-Christian he did not wish to take the oath of allegiance on the Bible. The law was on his side but his fellow MPs resisted his rights and caused him to be expelled. The picture shows him being arrested. They only gave in after a long fight, leaving Charles disillusioned about Parliament.

champion of people's rights, especially the right to their own beliefs. He was married but his wife had turned out to be a hopeless alcoholic. He made sure she was well looked after but he lived alone.

A relationship of equals

Charles Bradlaugh quickly recognised how bright and clever Annie was. He offered her a job on the Freethinker's paper. He gave her a lot of support, advice and encouragement, yet he treated her as an equal, something Frank had never done. Perhaps if things had been different, Charles and Annie would have married. They appear to have accepted that they could only be friends but for both of them it was probably the happiest and most productive friendship they ever had. She was thinking of their relationship when she wrote:

Charles Bradlaugh

'It will be a good thing for the world when a friendship between a man and a woman no longer means a protective condescension on one side and helpless dependence on the other but when they meet on equal ground.'

After all the turmoil and misery of the last few years Annie at last seemed to know where she was going. She had changed enormously in the seven years since her marriage. She had experienced deep unhappiness, had two children, undergone a complete change in her beliefs, left her husband, lost her mother — and survived as a woman alone. She had already stepped outside the traditional limits of behaviour. Now she flung herself into work as a militant anti-Christian and travelled up and down the

If the Bible and Religion stand in the way of women's rights then the Bible and Religion must go.

Annie Besant

country, giving speeches and holding meetings. This is how she described what drove her on:

> 'The desire to spread liberty and truer thought among men, to war against bigotry and superstition, to make the world freer and better than I found it — all this impelled me with a force that would not be denied.'

These two desires — to make the world a better place and to encourage the search for truth — lay behind all Annie's work, whether it was fighting for the right for women to practise birth control or for the right of Indian people to run their own country.

Annie and her mother. Mrs Wood died shortly after Annie left Frank, and Annie missed her love and understanding greatly. Mrs Wood had always worried that Annie was 'too religious'. Perhaps she would not have been surprised when Annie became a Theosophist.

The price of unrespectability

Annie was a great success among the Freethinkers. Her meetings were packed. Her reputation as a speaker grew steadily. But to the general public she was a scandalous woman who had left her husband and abandoned the Church. In spite of the fact that she supported women's rights, some women in the suffrage societies, who were fighting for the vote, did not accept her as one of them. Her anti-Christian views made her unrespectable — and respectability was very important to the (mainly middle-class) women of the movement. They remembered the experience of Mary Wollstonecraft, who had written an important book called *A Vindication of the Rights of Woman* about a hundred years earlier, in 1792. She had pointed out how society was organised to men's advantage and had argued for women's right to equal educational opportunities and voting powers.

Nobody before had explained women's position so well. However, Mary's unconventional personal life was used by critics to discredit her ideas. She had an illegitimate child and had attempted suicide. Many people then and later did not judge her work on its own merit. They drew parallels with her private life, of which they disapproved, saying that her ideas were as 'messy' and 'disorganised' as it was. However unfair they thought such attacks, many nineteenth century feminists felt that they had no choice but to conform to Victorian ideas of moral behaviour so that no man — or woman — could ever ridicule or attack their beliefs on the basis of their lifestyles. Annie was a threat to that respectability and many kept their distance.

She would have made a world famous leader for the Woman Suffrage movement . . . but by identifying herself with atheism, she'd gone too far.

Gertrude Williams,
The Passionate Pilgrim
(1932)

I had against me all the conventional beliefs and traditions of society in general, and I attacked them, not with bated breath and abundant apologies, but joyously and defiantly . . . no wonder I was denounced as an agitator, a firebrand and that all orthodox society turned up at me its most respectable nose.

Annie Besant,
An Autobiography

27

Chapter Five

The Fight for the Right to Birth Control

Annie thrived on work. Charles Bradlaugh's daughter Hypatia described how 'she could both write and study longer without rest . . . than any other person I have known'. As well as her work for the Freethinkers, she was writing other articles and book reviews. She was also involved in various other campaigns and gave speeches in support of striking miners and of poorly paid agricultural workers. Now she was earning more money, she was able to rent a house in St John's Wood, near Charles and his daughters. People talked, of course, and suggested that they were more than friends. Frank even had Annie followed by a private detective for a while, but there was never the slightest evidence of any 'immoral' behaviour.

A scandal breaks
Before long, however, Annie did do something truly scandalous for her society. She spoke out in public about birth control. Sex was generally discussed in hushed tones in Victorian days. Many a young wife suffered unnecessary misery simply because she knew so little about birth control, babies or even her own body. Annie was talking from bitter experience when she later wrote, 'Many an unhappy marriage dates from its very beginning, from the terrible shock to a young girl's sensitive modesty and pride, her helpless bewilderment and fear.' Women were encouraged to think of themselves as

'purer' than men. Wives were expected to tolerate unfaithful husbands, who were merely satisfying their coarser but 'natural' impulses.

Sex was associated with sin and shame and many people who were prepared to campaign for women's rights in politics, education or employment preferred not to have anything to do with a woman's right to birth control. Advice on contraception was hard to find and expensive. Marriage in Annie's time meant for most women — rich or poor — a succession of pregnancies. Annie herself was pregnant with Mabel too soon after Digby's birth and had quarrelled with Frank over the issue of birth control. Annie knew, from her visits to poor working women, just how much of a strain endless pregnancies placed on their health and happiness. Many a family

The people who worked in the profitable Victorian industries usually lived in damp, overcrowded slums. The women's health and strength was worn away by endless pregnancies and childcare and, when desperate, dangerous abortions. Contraceptive devices and information were very hard to get hold of and usually expensive.

CHURCH LANE
BLOOMSBURY

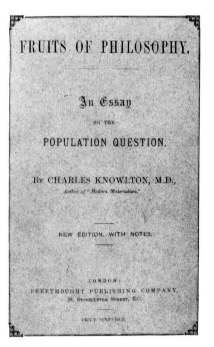

Annie knew how much working women suffered from the lack of information about birth control. She and Charles Bradlaugh deliberately printed The Fruits of Philosophy *at a price working women could afford.*

was reduced to poverty because they had too many mouths to feed. Mothers worn out by childbirth forced themselves back to work as soon as possible. Families crowded into one or two rooms knew no peace and lost any sense of dignity or pride.

On trial

In 1876 a printing colleague of Annie and Charles was fined for publishing a pamphlet called *The Fruits of Philosophy* by Dr Knowlton. The title was misleading. It actually contained information and advice about birth control. Since Charles and Annie believed strongly in people's right to have such information, they set up as printers themselves and in 1877 reprinted it — at a price even working-class women could afford. About five hundred of the pamphlets were sold on the first day. Within weeks they had been arrested and were put on trial for publishing an 'indecent' book which would 'corrupt' the morals of young people. Annie stood up in court and defended herself, which was almost unheard of for a woman at the time. The trial attracted a lot of attention. Annie said she was not only defending herself but was speaking on behalf of the poor, who did not have a voice: 'the fathers, who see their wage ever reducing . . . the mothers worn out with over-frequent childbearing . . . the little ones half starved because there is food enough for two but not enough for twelve.

She quoted the words of mothers who lived in fear of the next pregnancy, who suffered illness and were made old before their time. She spoke of crowded slums, where children had miserable lives, lacking sufficient food, fresh air, clothing or education. Many babies died in infancy.

Wasn't it better to prevent their birth than allow them to die later because of the terrible conditions they were born into, she asked.

Annie's defence was impressive. Even *The Times* congratulated her on her 'remarkable ability . . . and evident sincerity'. Charles spoke well too and when the jury went off to consider their verdict Annie and Charles felt hopeful. However, they won only half a victory. The jury agreed that the accused had not intended to corrupt the public — but they felt that the book's contents meant that it would do so. It was a confusing situation and the judge had to pronounce them guilty. Annie and Charles were determined to appeal. They faced the prospect of six months in prison and a fine of £100 — no small sum at the time, when a civil servant's family could expect to live on an annual income of £200. They took the case to the Court of Appeal, where the sentence was dropped. Victory was theirs at last.

The widespread publicity about the trial had a dramatic effect. The English birth rate dropped sharply from 1877, not least because the subject was at last brought out into the open and discussed. Even so, medical and government opposition to birth control continued and it wasn't until fifty years later that Marie Stopes opened her first clinic.

The price of victory

Newspapers had reported the story in great detail, some taking the side of Annie and Charles. Questions were asked in Parliament and plans were made to try to change the law on the teaching of birth control. The following year the world's first birth control clinic — in Holland — was opened. The trial had succeeded in bringing the issue out into the open. It was also a victory for the freedom of the press.

After the trial Annie wrote her own birth control pamphlet, which sold very well. Perhaps she would have been disappointed if she could have looked into the future. Fifty years later, the battle was still being fought. Only gradually was the secrecy around the subject broken down. Marie Stopes opened her first clinic in 1921. It was soon followed by others. However, it wasn't until the late 1960s that all local authorities had to provide a family planning service.

Nevertheless, Annie's work was a turning point in the history of birth control. The fact that it took so long for her ideas to be accepted shows how far ahead of her time she was. It took a great deal of bravery for a woman to stand up and fight over an issue which most men didn't dare support in public. She knew it would mean 'the loss of the pure reputation I prized, the good name I had guarded'. She paid a high price for her courage. It set her even further apart from the woman's movement of her time but more tragically, Annie was to be separated from her daughter because of it.

Had it been published at a guinea a copy, thus restricting the sales to a very small minority of the wealthy, the law would not have interfered . . . But the sale of a birth control manual at sixpence, and its clarity and simplicity, made all the difference. The working classes . . . could be informed about and emancipated from unwanted pregnancy.

S. Chandrasekhar,
A Dirty Filthy Book

Chapter Six

Personal Battles

Digby still lived with his father but Frank wanted Mabel too. Undoubtedly he now felt much bitterness towards Annie. Perhaps some of his motive was to hurt her. But he also genuinely feared the idea of his daughter being brought up in a 'godless' household. He was horrified when Mabel admitted that

Annie paid a high price for her brave decision to print the birth control pamphlet. Frank argued that this 'obscene' act, plus her 'heretical' anti-Christian views made her unfit to be a mother — and the courts agreed. Mabel was taken away. Annie was devastated.

What that trial and its results cost me in pain no-one but myself will ever know; on the other hand, there was the passionate gratitude evinced by letters from thousands of poor married women — thanking and blessing me.

Annie Besant,
An Autobiography

MABEL EMILY BESANT.
DEPRIVED OF HER MOTHER, MAY 23, 1878,
BY ORDER OF SIR GEORGE JESSEL, MASTER OF THE ROLLS,
ON ACCOUNT OF THAT MOTHER'S HERESY.

she was not expected to say her prayers every night nor was she even being taught any by her mother.

Frank was also shocked by his wife's court case. Her public speeches about contraception were the last straw. He fought for custody of Mabel on the grounds that Annie not only did not believe in God but she had also published an 'obscene' pamphlet. She was, he claimed, not fit to be a mother.

The court battle went on for months. Eventually, in spite of many witnesses who stated how well Annie looked after Mabel, she lost the case. Mabel was taken away almost immediately. The judge ruled that the two children could write to her; that she could see them once a month; that they could visit her twice a year and that they could spend one holiday together, provided a chaperone chosen by Frank was there too. It wasn't long before Annie realised that her short visits were upsetting Mabel so much that they did more harm than good. She gently and sadly withdrew from their young lives and decided to wait 'until they were old enough to understand and to judge for themselves' with whom they wished to live.

Annie was very bitter about this episode. At one point she remarked, 'It's a pity there isn't a God . . . It would do one so much good to hate Him.' Later she admitted that Frank's success in claiming that she was unfit to be a mother because she was not a Christian, had made her even more anti-religion. It seemed to her that 'it was Christianity which had robbed me of my child, and I struck mercilessly at it in return.' The pamphlets she wrote at this time were particularly fierce in their attacks on the Church.

Mabel was the sweetness and joy of my life . . . she gave [me] something to love and to tend, and thus gratified one of the strongest impulses of my nature.

Annie Besant,
An Autobiography

34

A mother's rights

Once again, Annie found her personal fight had become a public one. Many people felt it was wrong to deprive a parent of a child because of their beliefs. In newspapers and meetings there was much discussion over the right 'for freedom of opinion'. The courts never separated a parent and child in similar circumstances again. Frank's success had also shown up how helpless a married woman was in law. As Annie pointed out, if she had not been married to Frank, her children would have 'belonged' to her. As a wife, she had no rights. 'If you are legally your husband's wife, you can have no legal claim to your children; if legally you are your husband's mistress, your rights as a mother are secure.'

Annie was one of the first women to study for a degree. She attended London University, which opened its doors to women earlier than most (1878). In 1897 rioting Cambridge students (below) hung banners and effigies of women from the university buildings as a protest against admitting women.

Taking a degree

A learned or even over-accomplished woman is one of the most intolerable monsters in creation.

Dr Hodgson, nineteenth-century educationalist

Throughout the legal battles of 1878 and 1879, Annie was continuing to lecture and write on many subjects, including politics in India and Ireland. She was busier than most people, yet she found it was not enough to distract her from worrying about her children. Taking advantage of some changes in university rules, she decided to do a degree as well. A few years earlier this would have been impossible. London University had only just, in 1878, agreed to allow women to take degrees. Annie decided to study Science. She did extremely well. However, she kept failing one exam — practical chemistry — and this meant she was never awarded the full degree. It is not entirely unlikely that she was the victim of prejudice and that the examiners deliberately failed her. Women were only just breaking into higher education and many university men were still deeply opposed to the idea.

One example of the unpleasant way Annie was sometimes treated was the fact that she was refused permission to visit the Botanical Gardens in Regent's Park. This was after she had become the first woman in Britain to get first class honours in the Botany exam. She was clearly a serious student. The curator's excuse was that his daughters walked in the gardens and he did not wish them to meet such a scandalous woman! Birkbeck, the London University college she attended, deliberately left her name off their lists of successful exam results. They said people considering giving them funds might be put off if they realised she was a student there. Annie's work, especially for birth control and against the Church, had placed her outside respectable society and people were not going

Every effort to improve the education of women which presumes that they may . . . study the same subjects as their brothers and be measured by the same standards, does something towards lifting them out of the state of listless despair into which so many fall.

Emily Davies, nineteenth-century educational pioneer

to let her forget it. In a way, she was becoming the martyr that she had once dreamed of being when she was a girl. But of course the causes for which she was now suffering were anything but religious as the Victorian Church saw it.

Annie was not alone in questioning many of society's traditions and limitations. It was the actions of some other determined women, especially Emily Davies, which had persuaded universities to open their doors. The Time Chart on page 62 shows you some of the steps forward women were taking in the fight for equal rights in law, politics, employment and education.

In spite of the women's impressive academic results, many men remained opposed for a long time to the idea of female students. This reference to 'sweet girl graduates' gives some idea of the patronising attitudes women often encountered.

"SWEET GIRL GRADUATES"—THE VICE-CHANCELLOR (SIR JAMES PAGET) CONFERRING DEGREES AT LONDON UNIVERSITY

Chapter Seven

The Political Agitator

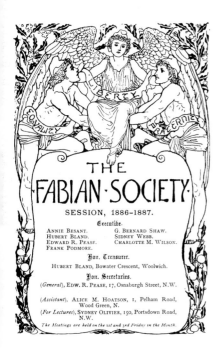

Annie was very busy, yet throughout this time she was also reflecting on political ideas. In 1884 she went to a meeting which left her very thoughtful. It was a debate about Socialism. Socialists believed that the country's wealth belonged to everyone, not just to the privileged and rich few who owned the farmland, factories, mines and businesses in which the mass of people worked. For some time she listened to their arguments and read as much as she could about Socialism but kept her ideas to herself. Yet the more she thought about it, the more sense it made to her. She felt that so much of the misery of the working class was because of the way they were exploited by the rich, who did not share their profits equally.

During this time she had become friendly with George Bernard Shaw. He was later a successful playwright but when Annie met him, he was young, unknown and struggling to pay his bills. He was a Fabian, which was a moderate branch of Socialism. Fabians believed in gradual change, not in revolution. Together he and Annie discussed her political ideas and doubts. Annie offered him some much needed paid writing work. It seems that Annie became very fond of Bernard Shaw while he clearly felt both respect and affection for her. He understood her better than most people. He had the sense of humour which Annie rather lacked. He made jokes about her energy, saying that any men who tried to keep pace with her 'usually

The chief fault of her extraordinary qualities was that she was fiercely proud . . . though I succeeded in sometimes making her laugh at me, I never succeeded in making her laugh at herself.

George Bernard Shaw on Annie Besant

collapsed and added the burden of nursing them to her already superhuman labours'. Fond as he was of Annie, he was rather alarmed at the thought of any more romantic involvement and made this clear when it seemed she might have wished for this.

In 1885 Annie formally joined the Fabians. This was not like joining the Socialists today. Their ideas were unacceptable to most of Victorian society. Many of her critics, then and later, implied that Annie was greatly influenced by Shaw and did not really make the decision herself. She was accused of 'having a mind like a milkjug', into which others poured their ideas. Behind all this lay the theory that women did not have minds of their own — they just followed those of the latest man in their life. Yet not only had Annie thought hard and long about Socialism but she was also a woman of great bravery who had already stood up for her own ideas time after time, even losing custody of her child because of her beliefs. Annie was scornful of such attacks. As she said,

George Bernard Shaw was a good friend of Annie's, especially during her socialist days. He liked and admired her but felt she sometimes took things too seriously. He modelled Raina, in his play Arms and the Man, *on Annie and her 'noble attitude and thrilling voice'.*

> 'The moment a man uses a woman's sex to discredit her arguments, the thoughtful reader knows that he is unable to answer the arguments themselves. But really these silly sneers at a woman's ability have lost their force, and are best met with a laugh at the stupendous "male self-conceit" of the writer.'

In the front line

Annie took a little time to find her role in Socialism. Her personality made it hard to take a back seat or to spend hours in meetings quietly discussing plans and routine matters. She wanted to be out there

Bloody Sunday, 13 November 1887. Annie assisted many of the unemployed marchers who were injured or arrested after the event. Soon afterwards she and W. T. Stead, a journalist, founded The Link. *It was to expose social injustice and act as a voice for the poor and exploited.*

fighting the system, rousing people's emotions and spurring them on to activity. As Shaw described it, she became a sort of one-woman 'expeditionary force, always to the front when there was trouble or danger, carrying away audiences for us . . . founding branches for us throughout the country, dashing into the great strikes and free speech agitations . . .'

There was a lot to be done. In the 1880s the country's economy was not doing well. Many people were thrown into unemployment. By the autumn of 1887, the situation was worse. A cold and hungry winter loomed ahead. The unemployed held meetings and marches, hoping to make the government do something about their suffering. On 13 November, known thereafter as Bloody Sunday, a mass demonstration in Trafalgar Square was broken up by policemen on horses. It was a chaotic and violent scene.

Over a hundred people were injured and two people killed. Another hundred or so were imprisoned.

Annie threw all her energy into helping those in jail and protesting against the way the government and the police had behaved. She worked with a journalist called W. T. Stead, who was well known for his articles exposing injustices and scandals in society. Together they founded a paper called *The Link*. It was to speak for the poor and the exploited — 'the despairing silent ones' — just as Annie had when she had made history and pleaded in court for the right of poor women to have access to birth control.

Annie was soon to play a major part in another landmark event, this time in the history of trade unions. It was triggered off by an article she wrote for *The Link* called 'White Slavery in London'. It was about the terrible working conditions of women employed in Bryant and May's match factory in the East End of London.

The Link, *a journal which has been founded . . . simply and solely as the helper of the helpless, the friend of the oppressed, and the advocate and champion of the cause of the Disinherited of our race.*

Annie Besant and W. T. Stead in the first issue of The Link, *February 1888.*

A Journal for the Servants of Man.

REGISTERED FOR]   [TRANSMISSION ABROAD.

No. 37.   SATURDAY, OCTOBER 13, 1888.   ONE HALFPENNY.

Chapter Eight

The Match Girls' Strike

When Annie had visited the factory she was horrified by what she saw. Many of the workers were teenage girls, who often worked from 6.30 a.m. to 6 p.m. Their pay averaged four shillings a week, less than the rent of one room. Most of them survived on bread, butter and tea. They could not afford anything else. The work itself was dirty and dangerous. The ends of the matches were dipped in phosphorus, a chemical which gave off poisonous fumes. These seeped into the girls' teeth and jawbones and caused them to rot. This horrible condition was known as 'phossy jaw'. On top of this, the owners used to fine the girls for such offences as having dirty feet or being untidy.

Many middle-class people owned shares in factories like this one. They made money from the girls' hard work but the workers never got any pay rises. In her article, Annie tried to make the shareholders see what they were allowing the girls — who might have been the same age as their own daughters — to suffer.

'Do you know that girls are used to carry boxes on their heads until the hair is rubbed off and the young heads are bald at fifteen years of age? Country clergymen with shares in Bryant and May's, draw down on your knee your fifteen-year-old daughter; pass your hand . . . over the silky, clustering curls, rejoice . . . in the thick, shiny tresses. Then, like a ghastly

Born in slums, driven to work while still children, undersized because underfed, oppressed because helpless, flung aside as soon as worked out, who cares if they die or go on the streets, provided only that the Bryant and May shareholders get their twenty-three per cent?

Annie Besant on the match girls, 'White Slavery', The Link

vision, let there rise before you the pale, wan face of another man's fifteen year old daughter.'

The managers of Bryant and May said the article was nonsense. They sacked the girls who had given her information about their work. Then they tried to force the others to sign a statement saying that what Annie had

The matchmakers, many of them girls in their teens, were the first unskilled workers to strike successfully. They inspired other women workers and unskilled labourers to unite and fight to improve their often wretched conditions.

written was untrue and that they were happy in their work. The girls refused. Annie was furious at the management. 'Why not sue me for libel and disprove my statement in open court if they can,' she asked, 'instead of threatening to throw these children out into the streets?' She held a protest meeting and in July 1888, 1400 of them went on strike. It was a very brave thing to do, since they were already on the poverty line. They had no union, so there was no strike pay. Trade unions at this time were mainly for skilled male workers who were better paid.

The spark turns into a fire

A reporter from *The Star*, a London paper, visited the strikers on the first morning. 'Is this all true,' he asked, 'that Mrs Besant has been writing?' 'Yes,' they replied, 'all . . . was true and we'd have come out long since, but we weren't agreed.' The factory manager told a different story and explained the strike by saying that 'I have no doubt that they have been influenced by the twaddle of Mrs Besant and other Socialists.' *The Times* supported the management, commenting that 'the match girls have not been suffered to take their own course, but have been egged on to strike by irresponsible advisers.'

Together with the match girls who 'kept brave and bright all through', Annie whipped up a lot of support for their case. People gave money to keep them going through the strike. Bryant and May failed to prove that Annie's article was 'nothing but a tissue of lies', as they had claimed. Newspapers wrote articles sympathetic to the strikers. Charles Bradlaugh, by now an MP, raised the matter in Parliament. The company directors were up against not only the match girls and Annie

Besant but increasing public support. Bryant and May caved in. They agreed to improve the working conditions. Before too long, the factory had become a model workplace with an independent union. It was a tremendous victory, not just for women workers, but for all unskilled workers. It showed that if they joined together, they could have considerable power and win important battles for their rights. Unions were no longer just for skilled male workers.

After the victory of the match girls' strike, Annie campaigned hard for improved conditions for other workers. Tramping the streets of London's East End, she visited

Box-making in London's East End. Sweated labour continued, especially amongst home workers, who were usually poor women unable to leave their small children and desperate for money. They were especially vulnerable to exploitation because it was so hard for them to band together in demands for fairer wages.

I believe poverty is the result of ignorance and of bad social arrangements, and that therefore it may be eradicated by knowledge and by social change . . . but we grudge every halfpenny that increases the education rate and howl down every proposal to build decent houses for the poor.

Annie Besant

For these child martyrs of the slums . . . society has only formulas, not food.

Annie Besant, arguing for the provision of free school meals

overcrowded homes and factories where women and children sewed clothes, assembled match boxes, pulled fur from animal skins, and made boots, toys, cigarettes and other goods. These 'sweatshops' were terribly unhealthy places, with no fresh air, proper lighting or safety controls. Hours were long, wages were low and the workers usually had to buy their own materials. She also talked to printers, dockers, gas workers, house-painters, transport workers and others. She supported them in any way she could, whether by giving advice and information or help with organisation, publicity or fund-raising. Above all, Annie wrote and spoke out on behalf of these people all over the country. She was determined to make the middle classes see the silent misery which often lay behind their wealth and comfort.

Free school meals

Yet another cause was beginning to take up her time. Annie had wanted to become a member of London's County Council but she discovered women were not allowed. So she decided to stand for election to the London School Board in Tower Hamlets. Boards were the committees responsible for running state schools. Since 1870 all local authorities had to provide schools and in 1880 education was made compulsory for all children up to ten.

Annie wanted to bring in free school meals, knowing how under-nourished and weak many poor children were and how hard this made it for them to concentrate. Because she was against compulsory religious education, many churchmen opposed her election but her popularity was high in the East End, where she had helped so many people. She won more votes than anyone else. Once she was on the Board, she made changes which some people still regard as the best things she ever did. She not only introduced school meals, but she also started off the idea of school medical services. She did not forget her trade union principles either. She made sure that contracts for anything the Board needed to buy for the schools were only given to firms which obeyed union rules and which paid their workers a fair wage. This was an important step forward, for it meant public organisations were now supporting trade union ideas.

'Clemming Versus Cramming'

This Punch *cartoon illustrates something Annie knew was a serious problem. Many children in state schools were badly underfed, which made it hard to concentrate. When she joined the London School Board, Annie introduced free school meals and medical treatment. Many regard this as one of the most important achievements of her varied career.*

('Clemming' means to waste away from hunger.)

Chapter Nine

Finding the Light

The symbol of Theosophy, incorporating those of the major world religions.

Annie had achieved a lot. Yet the few who knew her well felt she was not really happy. Since Mabel had been taken away, it seemed Annie often used work as a means to forget her worries and got less enjoyment from it. Annie was still a very spiritual person. She might have rejected Christianity but she still sought answers for what she called 'the riddle of life and mind'. Why do people have to suffer? What are we here for? What happens when we die?

> 'Oh, those trudges through the lanes and alleys round Bethnal Green Junction late at night, when our day's work was over; children lying about on shavings, rags, anything; famine looking out of baby faces, out of women's eyes, out of the tremulous hands of men . . . ever louder sounded the question, "Where is the cure for sorrow, what the way of rescue for the world?"'

Socialism had seemed to offer an explanation for much of the misery she saw around her in city slums and poor villages. Yet it was not enough.

> 'Ever more and more had been growing on me the feeling that something more than I had was needed for the cure of social ills. The Socialist position suffced on the economic side, but where to gain the inspiration, the motive, which should lead to the realisation of the Brotherhood of

Man? Our efforts to really organise bands of unselfish workers had failed. Much indeed had been done, but there was not a real movement of self-sacrificing devotion, in which men worked for Love's sake only, and asked but to give, not to take.'

Annie was looking for more than just political or economic answers. She was searching for a movement which united people from love rather than self-interest. She believed there was 'some hidden thing, some hidden power' which would reveal the Truth about life. In 1889, in her early forties, she felt she had at last found it.

Theosophy

In 1889 W. T. Stead gave her a book to review called *The Secret Doctrine*. It changed her life. Although it was long and difficult to read, Annie was 'dazzled' and 'all my puzzles, riddles, problems seemed to disappear . . . I knew the weary search was over and the very Truth was found.'

The Secret Doctrine was written by Helena Blavatsky, leader of the Theosophical Society. Theosophists drew their beliefs from ideas contained within the ancient Eastern religions of Hinduism and Buddhism. Indeed, they believed that all religions were variations of an earlier universal Wisdom. They believed in rebirth and that people are part of a cycle of life in which each existence brings them closer to the highest spiritual levels. At the very top are the Masters, totally spiritual beings with whom Helena and others were able to communicate.

Helena Blavatsky was a strange woman who had led a colourful life. Born in Russia, she had travelled all over the world. She had

I have been told that I plunged headlong into Theosophy and let my enthusiasm carry me away. I think the charge is true, in so far as the decision was swiftly taken; but it had long been led up to . . . and more than all I hoped for in that first plunge has been realised.

Annie Besant,
An Autobiography

a vivid imagination and a powerful personality. After reading her book, Annie arranged to meet her. She found herself almost unwillingly impressed by this cultured woman, who weighed over sixteen stone and was regally wheeled about in a huge wheelchair. Annie studied criticisms of Theosophy which showed that Helena had sometimes used magical trickery to impress her audiences. Annie herself had been unfairly criticised for her beliefs and actions too often to take much notice of public disapproval or suspicion of Helena. In the end she felt quite certain that the philosophy of Theosophy held the Truth for which she had been searching for so long. She publically declared herself a Theosophist, although she knew that this was likely to make herself a

Helena Blavatsky, founder of the Theosophical Society. Theosophy stands for 'Divine Wisdom', the Truth which Theosophists believe lies behind all the world's different religions. They describe it as 'the light which shines through the many coloured lamps of religion . . . the thread of truth in scriptures, creeds, symbols, myths and rituals'.

target of 'ridicule — worse than hatred'. She was right.

Most of her friends were horrified. Charles Bradlaugh was sad and disillusioned that the woman with whom he had shared so many ideas now believed in 'matters which seem to me as unreal as it is possible for any fiction to be'. George Bernard Shaw was 'staggered' and felt it meant 'the loss of a powerful colleague and of a friendship which had become part of my daily life.' Many people, then and now, have found it hard to understand how Annie, the clear-sighted campaigner for social reform, could become the high priestess of Theosophy, a believer in messages from Masters and Messiahs. (In 1909 the Society chose a young Indian boy, Krishnamurti, to be the New Christ or Messiah.) Yet we must remember that Annie, who was so far ahead of her time in many of her ideas, was a true Victorian in her need for some spiritual framework and explanation of life. Without it, she felt very lost. Having rejected Christianity and worked through Freethought and Socialism, she never stopped searching for a belief which would make greater sense of life. For her, Theosophy was the answer. It was, like Christianity, rooted in the past, indeed in very ancient beliefs, yet seemed to be without the narrowness and the stern and forbidding face of Victorian Christianity. And Theosophy was very popular at this time, for there was a lot of interest in spiritualism, the occult and religions of the East. Theosophy's connection with Eastern religions changed Annie's life in a further dramatic way. It was to take her to India, which she would come to regard as her true home and where she would live for most of the rest of her life.

This cartoon makes fun of Annie's association with Helena Blavatsky and Mahatma Gandhi. Annie was often accused of being inconsistent, swayed by others and switching from one interest to another. Yet if a man had covered her range of activity and achievement, he would probably have been complimented on being a 'renaissance man' with an inquiring and intelligent mind.

Peace

Once Annie believed in something, as we have seen, she was single-minded in her devotion to it, however unpopular it might make her. Over the next couple of years, she left the Fabians and the London School Board, and mainly lectured and wrote on Theosophy. She offered her house as the Society's headquarters. She quickly became one of the most important leaders of the movement. Although she was growing further and further apart from her old friends, they could see that her new beliefs were at last bringing her some contentment. Her happiness increased when Mabel and Digby, now nineteen and twenty-one, joined her. As she had hoped, once they were old

Annie with some of her Indian colleagues and the young Krishnamurti and his brother. Krishnamurti was adopted as a boy by the Theosophists and groomed for his future role as the Messiah or World Teacher.

enough to make up their own minds, they left Frank for their mother.

Helena Blavatsky was delighted with her new disciple. She understood Annie well. She recognised that her own rather showbusiness-like style was different from Annie's, who took everything so seriously. Annie was, she said, 'the soul of honour and uncompromisingly truthful'. In 1891 Helena died. Annie became head of the society in Europe and India. Two years later, in her mid-forties, she took the long sea voyage east. Annie had long been interested in Indian affairs but when she arrived there it was not politics but Indian culture and religious ideas which fascinated her most. She felt she had found her true spiritual home. She grew to love the country and the people deeply and was to spend most of the second half of her life there.

When she returned from this first visit, she faced one of the scandals which every now and then occurred in the Theosophical Society. There were accusations of forged letters and all sorts of lies. The Society seemed to have attracted a few rather shady characters whose attitude to truth was not the same as Annie's. She was not good at seeing through these sort of people. Even when their dishonesty was revealed she did not deal with them effectively, partly out of loyalty and partly because she was never very good at admitting she had been wrong. Some of the Society's troubles got into the newspapers. Cartoons about them were published. It was a difficult time for Annie. She was a fighter and totally committed to Theosophy but these battles within the Society and against bad publicity were not the sort of battles she enjoyed.

Combative on the platform in defence of any cause I cared for, I shrink from quarrel or disapproval in the home, and am a coward at heart in private . . . How often have I passed unhappy quarters of an hour screwing up my courage to find fault with some subordinate whom my duty compelled me to reprove.

Annie Besant,
An Autobiography

Chapter Ten

An Indian Summer

An extraordinary woman, Irish by birth, English by manner, Indian by adoption.

Hindoo Patriot, *26 May 1917*

By 1907 Annie was President of the Society and spending more and more time in India. She adopted Indian dress and habits and made her home there. She did a great deal to encourage Indians to once again take pride in their own religion and culture, calling on 'the youths of India' to 'act up to the traditions of their past, instead of fawning on a foreign power'. India at this time was a colony of Britain and had been for many years. The British had frequently organised India's trade to their own advantage. For example, India's cotton and silk industries, which had once produced some of the finest cloth in the world, were neglected and run down. Meanwhile British textiles had taken their place and were being sold in India and other foreign markets. From being a wealthy nation, India had become one of the poorest countries in the world. Indians were treated as inferiors and were banned from certain organisations and jobs by the British.

Annie knew how this treatment could break the spirit of a nation. She left politics alone and concentrated on founding schools and colleges and encouraging the study of Indian philosophy, religion, literature and arts because she believed this was the only way to revive 'the greatness of India, and the happiness of her people'. She campaigned for social reforms, including better rights for Indian women. Yet, as she got more deeply involved in raising India's sense of national pride, she inevitably became drawn into politics again.

Indian cotton being shipped to England, where it was woven into textiles and sold back to India. In this way India's own textile industry, once world famous, had seriously declined. Annie spoke out against this 'destruction of India's trade'.

From 1913 onwards, she increasingly argued in articles and speeches for India's right to self-government, or Home Rule. This meant giving Indians more power in how their country was run. She claimed that the British rulers of India were 'crushing the life out of the people'. They had broken promises and ignored the needs of Indians. She warned, however, that there was 'a limit to the patience of a nation and that limit is very nearly reached in India'. She believed that if the British started treating Indians as equals they could 'win back the love of India . . . She does not trust you today . . . Realise that India is a civilised nation, a mighty nation with a past that no nation in the world can equal.'

Annie was not denying Britain's right to rule an Empire. She lived in an age in which few questioned this. Indeed, she argued that 'It is India which makes Britain an Empire' and so to destroy the old relationship between the two countries would be a terrible mistake. But she was ahead of her time in arguing for India's right to self-government

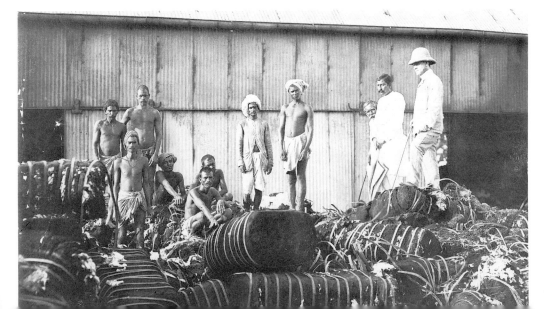

under Britain. Even Theosophists disagreed with her, however much they respected the ancient beliefs of India.

Internment

In 1914 the First World War broke out. Annie agreed that India should help Britain but she did not stop arguing for Home Rule. This made her popular in India but very unpopular with the British government. Feelings against British rule were growing in India. Mahatma Gandhi had begun his campaign of non-violent resistance. More and more Indians joined in marches and meetings. They protested against having to buy British goods rather than those made in India. By 1917 feelings were running high. It was decided that Annie should be 'interned' for the rest of the war, as a way of keeping her quiet. She was sent to a beautiful hill town called Ootacamund. Annie was nearly

When Annie was interned by the British in 1917, there was a great outcry by the Indian people for her release. This photograph shows her being triumphantly paraded through the streets and welcomed back by cheering crowds.

seventy. Most seventy-year-olds might have found staying somewhere so quiet and cool a relief. But without the bustle and challenge of her work, Annie was quite lost. As one biographer (Rosemary Dinnage) has said, 'Work had been her drug and now she was deprived of it.' It is ironic that Annie, who so loved and respected Indian religious philosophy, never managed to achieve the inner peace which is so important a part of it.

People protested so much about Annie's internment that the governors were forced to release her. She rushed back into the whirl and excitement of political activity and was rewarded by one of the greatest honours of her career. She was elected President of the Indian National Congress. That India should elect a white person and a woman to this most important political position showed the respect they had for her.

If people, and there are hundreds and thousands of them among our countrymen, feel a pang of genuine regret at her internment, it is because, whether they agree with or differ from her in her political or religious views, they know she loves India with a whole hearted love.

Hindoo Patriot 23 June 1917

Final years

Annie's year as President was a mixed triumph. The mood was changing fast in India. Gandhi was becoming far more popular. He appealed to the mass of ordinary people in India. They could identify with him in a way they couldn't possibly with an elderly white woman. Annie had been most popular with a circle of educated Indians, but the movement for self-government had now become a wider, mass movement. And however much she 'felt' Indian, Annie was not. As an Indian writer said, she had 'inspired India's men and women to realise their own freedom'. But the price of her success was that she was no longer the right person to lead the movement for Indian independence. In many ways Annie understood this, however much it hurt her.

'All these forty years my white body has been an asset . . . It is no longer so, and the youth of India has become normal in its behaviour. My work has been crowned with success.'

Annie stayed on in India, working more in the background. She and Gandhi did not agree on many matters but he had far more power now. Although in her seventies, she still devoted much of her astonishing energy to running the Theosophical Society.

▶ From about 1918, Annie's influence declined as Mahatma Gandhi increasingly became the inspiration behind the Indian independence movement. He led the famous Salt March of 1930. By collecting salt deposits from an Indian beach, Gandhi and his supporters were defying one of the many laws and taxes which forced them to buy British rather than Indian goods.

Mahatma Gandhi.

A London Tribute

In 1924 she travelled to London for a celebration of her fifty years of public service. Colleagues and friends paid tribute to all she had achieved, saying 'how wonderfully she has been a forerunner of many things we now take in our national life as a natural course' (Margaret Bondfield). Free school meals, birth control clinics (which were at last opening up throughout England), improved working and living conditions for many unskilled workers, women taking degrees and entering professions such as science and law, better legal rights for separated or divorced mothers — all these improvements owed something to the work and ideas of Annie Besant. Even Gandhi was generous in his praise, saying 'I wish to express my admiration for this long record of service and the amazing energy and courage that lay behind it.' And although Gandhi was now the driving force behind Indian politics, her influence remained so strong that one journalist commented, 'Gandhi's only rival in India is a woman — perhaps the most remarkable of living women.'

Annie returned to India and continued

Krishnamurti

lecturing, writing and travelling. In 1929 there
was a great blow for the Theosophical
Society. Krishnamurti, now thirty-four years
old, left the Theosophists and rejected his
role as their Messiah. Annie must have been
very disappointed but she and Krishnamurti
continued to feel much affection and respect
for each other. He remained a deeply
spiritual man and began to preach his own
message.

In 1933 Annie died peacefully in Madras.
She was eighty-five. Newspapers in India and
England paid tribute to her and letters and
telegrams poured into Madras from friends
and colleagues. They were aware that they
had lost 'a great woman, a strong woman . . .
a person we cannot forget easily', as one of
her Indian colleagues later wrote.

Yet in some ways she was later rather
forgotten. Many school history books make
no mention of her. Even books dealing with
the women's movement tended to treat her
rather briefly. In India her memory is more
alive. Schools and colleges she helped to
found still exist. Indians still remember her
love of their country and her belief in the
people's right to be self-governing.

Perhaps one of the reasons that this
remarkable woman has been neglected is that
she was a pioneer in so many different areas.
She is not associated with one particular
cause as is Florence Nightingale and nursing,
or Mrs Pankhurst and the vote. Her story has
many themes, and many different successes
and failures. She even spent a large part of
her life living in and working for the rights of
another country. Perhaps another reason is
her Theosophy. Her unconventional beliefs
were difficult for many people to understand
or sympathise with. The talk of Messiahs and

messages from other beings has sometimes seemed just too odd for comfort to people who admired Annie in other ways.

Annie's story tells us much about the world she lived in. She questioned many of its limitations and injustices. She fought for change and her personal and public battles touched upon many different aspects of Victorian times. But she was a remarkable woman for any time. She was brave enough to face ridicule and anger for her beliefs. She could work harder and longer than almost all of her male and female colleagues. She was clever, an inspiring public speaker, and an efficient organiser. She perhaps took things too seriously. She hated admitting she was wrong and certainly was not very good at laughing at herself. But she was not only admired and respected, she was loved by many who knew her. She was utterly sincere in her desire to make the world she lived in a better place. She once wrote that the only words she wanted on her tombstone were 'She tried to follow truth'. It is this which perhaps explains the variety of her interests and achievements. The common thread which links the devoted disciple of Theosophy with the earlier, anti-religious political campaigner was her search for a truthful solution to 'the riddle of life and mind'.

TIME CHART

Events in Annie Besant's life

1847 Annie Wood born
1855 Annie joins Miss Marryat's school
1867 Annie marries Frank Besant
1869 Digby, their son, born
1871 Mabel, their daughter, born
1873 Annie rejects Christianity and leaves Frank, taking Mabel
1874 Annie meets Charles Bradlaugh, a Freethinker, and starts working for the National Secular Society
1877 Annie and Charles are put on trial for publishing a book giving information about birth control
1879 Annie is found by the courts to be an unfit mother and loses custody of Mabel
Annie studies for a degree in science
1855 Annie becomes a Socialist and joins the Fabian Society
1887 Bloody Sunday
Annie and W. T. Stead start *The Link*
1888 Annie helps the Match Girls of Bryant and May win their strike
She is elected to the London School Board
1889 Annie is converted to Theosophy
1891 Annie becomes leader of Theosophical Society in Europe and India
1893 First visit to India, which is to become her home
1907 Annie becomes President of the Theosophical Society
1909 Krishnamurti is chosen to be the Messiah
1913 Annie becomes involved in political work for India
1917 Annie is interned, released, and elected President of India's National Congress
1924 Tribute to her fifty years of public service takes place in London
1929 Krishnamurti leaves the Theosophical Society
1933 Annie dies, in Madras, India

Key dates in social reform (1857–1947)

1857 Matrimonial Causes Act: a wife deserted by her husband can keep any money she earns

1863 Girls allowed to take Cambridge Examination (equivalent to A level)

1869 First women's university college founded at Hitchin, later to become Girton, Cambridge

1870 Married Woman's Property Act: women living with their husbands can keep any money they earn
Education Act: all local authorities to provide schools
Women allowed to become members of School Boards

1875 Law passed allowing universities to grant women degrees

1878 London University opens degrees to women (the others refuse)

1880 Education Act: compulsory schooling for all children up to the age of ten

1882 Married Women's Property Act: married women can own property

1888 Women allowed to vote in local elections

1889 Women's Trade Union League founded

1897 National Union of Women's Suffrage Societies founded

1907 Qualification of Women Act: women can become local councillors

1918 All women householders over thirty get the vote

1919 Sex Disqualification Removal Act: women can become magistrates, jurors, barristers and solicitors

1921 Marie Stopes opens her first birth control clinic

1923 Matrimonial Causes Act: women can now divorce for the same reasons as men

1925 Guardianship of Infants Act: men and women have equal rights over their children

1928 Women in Britain gain the vote on equal terms with men

1947 India gains independence

Index

The publishers wish to thank the following for supplying photographs for this book:

BBC Hulton Picture Library cover left; pages 23, 24, 25, 26, 29, 35, 39, 43, 51; British Library page 30; British Newspaper Library page 41; Mary Evans Picture Library pages 9, 15, 16, 22, 40, 45, 60; *Illustrated London News* page 59; Mansell Collection pages 13, 14, 19, 33, 37, 47, 55, 58; Nehru Memorial Museum and Library, New Delhi page 52; Marie Stopes House page 31; The Theosophical Society in England cover right, pages 2, 6, 10, 17, 48, 50, 56, 61.

The author would like to thank Rosemary Auchmuty and Sue Adler for all their advice and encouragement – both for this book and for the series as a whole.

Further Reading

Annie Besant Rosemary Dinnage (Penguin, 1987)
The Match Girls' Strike Reg Beer (Labour Museum Pamphlet Number Two)
The First Five Lives of Annie Besant A. Nethercot (Rupert Hart-Davis, 1960)
The Last Four Lives of Annie Besant A. Nethercot (Rupert Hart-Davis, 1963)
An Autobiography Annie Besant, 1893
The Changing Status of Women Olivia Bennett (Bell & Hyman, 1987)